Sh
Day

a little book of the

Written & Illustrated by

Karen Cater

Published in Great Britain
by Hedingham Fair 2014

ISBN:978-0-9556475-7-4

Printed in Great Britain by
The Five Castles Press
Ipswich

www.hedinghamfair.co.uk

Contents

Chapter 1 Winter Solstice....................5
How does the Sun stand still?....................6
Understanding the annual cycle....................8
Measuring the cycle of the Sun....................10
Chapter 2 Neolithic Stones....................12
Stonehenge....................14
Callanish....................16
Newgrange....................18
Long Meg & her Daughters....................20
Rollright Stones....................22
Avebury....................24
Chapter 3 Celtic Wisdom....................26
Ogham, the Druid tree alphabet....................27
Tree wheel, the Ogham year....................28
Yew - a guardian at the threshold....................30
Scotts pine - a signpost into the new year....................32
Chapter 4 Mistletoe 'Allheal'....................34
The Golden Sickle....................36
The Kissing Bough....................38
Bring Mistletoe in....................40

Chapter 5 Evolution of Legends and Customs................42
Roman Saturnalia...42
The Other Roman Midwinter Festival.............................44
The Dark Ages, Heathens & Christian Missionaries........46
The Green Man...48
Deck the Halls with Boughs of Holly..............................49
Winter Solstice Green Man...50
The Holly King & the Oak King....................................52
The Mummers are Coming!..54
Mummers at Christmas...56
Here we Come a-Wassailing...58
Apple Orchard Wassailing..60
Helping to Revive the Sun..62

Chapter 1

WINTER SOLSTICE

What does that mean?

The word solstice comes from the Latin sol (sun) and sistere (to stand still). So the Winter Solstice is when the sun stands still in winter. What does this really mean?

As the earth rotates around the Sun (a full circuit takes one year), it is spinning, giving us day and night as the earth moves, first towards then away from the Sun. The axis on which the earth spins is tilted. When the earth tilts towards the sun, days become longer than nights and the weather is warmer (summer). In winter the earth tilts away: nights become longer than days and weather gets colder.

How does the Sun stand still?

In Britain, in summer, the Sun rises early in the morning in the north east, climbing high into the sky in a big arc, setting late in the evening in the north west. In winter the Sun rises later in the south east, climbs barely above the horizon and sets earlier in the south west.

As the annual cycle progresses between winter and summer and back to winter, the positions of the Sunrise and Sunset move gradually along the horizon and back again.

At the solstices the Sun 'stands still'. These are the two points in the year when sunrise and sunset are at their extreme positions on the horizon, each occurring at exactly the same point for 3 days before returning back along the horizon in the Sun's annual cycle. So the progress of the sunrise and sunset appears to stand still.

At these times the Sun also reaches its highest (midsummer) or lowest (midwinter) point in its daily circuit across the sky. Precise dates of solstices are mathematically calculated by astronomers as the exact moment when the direction reverses. They can vary from 20th to 22nd June (summer) or December (winter), though they most usually happen on 21st. So in most years the Winter Solstice is 21st December, and is the lowest ebb of the Sun's strength, when it barely rises only for a few hours and light and warmth are weakest.

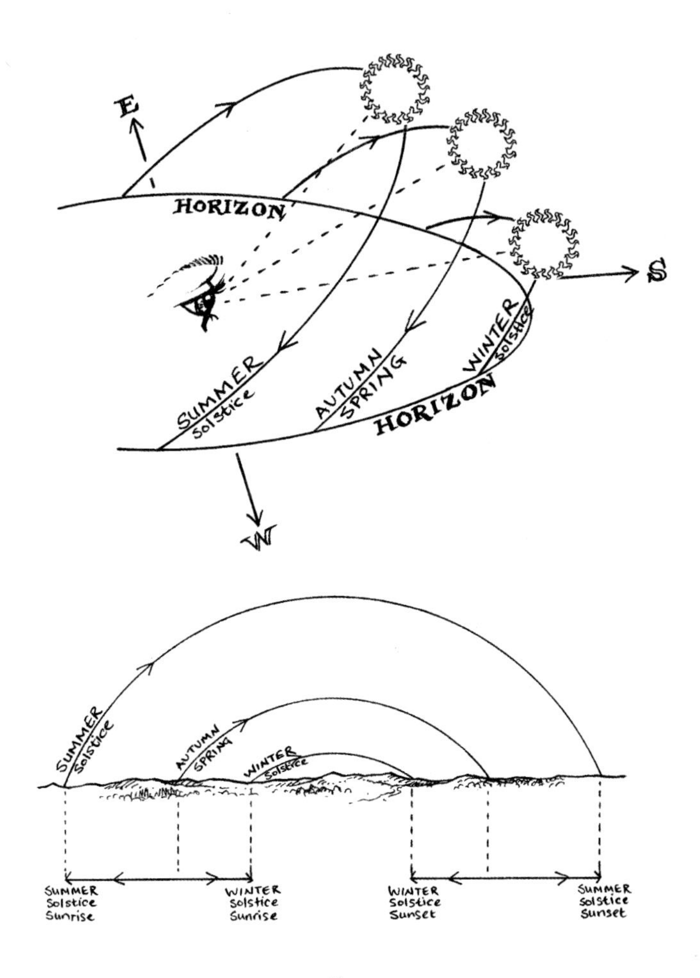
E
HORIZON
S
SUMMER
Solstice
AUTUMN
SPRING
WINTER
Solstice
HORIZON
W
SUMMER
Solstice
AUTUMN
SPRING
WINTER
Solstice
SUMMER
Solstice
Sunrise
WINTER
Solstice
Sunrise
WINTER
Solstice
Sunset
SUMMER
Solstice
Sunset

Understanding the Annual Cycle

In Britain, 7,000 years ago (around 5,000BC) the 'Neolithic Revolution' took place. This movement had already spread throughout most of the populated world. Peoples who for thousands of years had been hunter-gatherers began to settle in small communities and become farmers; domesticating animals and growing crops. For the first time people stayed in one place for generations, grew their food and so became more dependent upon the weather and the seasons for their survival. Neolithic people needed to understand the behaviour of these sometimes unpredictable forces of nature within the area they had settled. They hoped to gain some measure of control over their future wellbeing by studying the patterns of the annual cycle.

Over time people realised how the lands they inhabited interacted with the movements of celestial bodies. The rising and setting of Sun, Moon and Stars aligned with landmarks on their horizons. At midwinter, the Sun loses its strength, with both its warmth and light fading. In more northerly places it barely rises above the horizon. Perhaps people began to think it might help the Sun return to its former strength if the whole community got together and performed some kind of ritual of sympathetic magic, maybe with fire and light. But first they needed to know when the lowest ebb of the Sun's strength would occur.

A modern representation of the Wheel of the Year showing seasonal variations in the natural world, together with the eight festivals of the Celtic year.

Measuring the Cycle of the Sun

To record the different points on the horizon at which the Sun rose and set each day, marker poles or stones could be positioned in line with a static feature, a tree or rock, giving a diagrammatical representation on the land, which could be used as a calendar. This must have taken many years to complete as cloudy skies must have spoiled the observations sometimes for weeks on end.

Recording the movements of the Sun was reasonably simple as its annual cycle was the same every year, but when the Moon was studied it became obvious that this would be far more complicated. Not only did the Moon have an obvious monthly cycle, its journeys around the sky followed another cycle lasting nearly nineteen years, before eventually returning to its original position. Imagine the lifetime of constant observing, measuring and recording that must have been necessary to work out these lunar cycles, especially as they would have to do it all several times to be sure of the pattern!

As people learned from their observations, only a small leap of imagination was needed to transform measurements into permanent structures, capable not only of recording, but predicting celestial events. By standing at the central observation point and watching the sunrise / sunset, it could be calculated how many days there would be until the solstice.

Once it became possible to predict the Winter Solstice, its alignment could be built into all manner of new wonders. At Newgrange in Ireland, a chambered tomb was constructed with a tiny window that let in the first rays of the Winter Solstice sunrise to fall upon a wall decorated with ornate carvings at other times hidden in deep gloom. It may have been believed that the Sun was fertilising the Earth Mother with the power of light, piercing the darkness of the tomb/womb, and returning life and light to the land. What magic that must have seemed!

Chapter 2

NEOLITHIC STONES

As the Neolithic age progressed, ideas evolved. Stone circles were built on windswept hilltops or on wide plains, varying in size and complexity. Some were simple circles, perhaps with an outlier stone to mark the alignment. Others had many alignments built into a more complicated plan, culminating in the massive and complex Stonehenge, which took over 1500 years to complete (3150 – 1500BC). Stonehenge started as a circular earthwork bank and ditch (henge). There was a stone on either side of the entrance, with post holes dotted around recording the rise of the full moon around midwinter. Later this entrance was widened, and the 'Heel stone' added, which aligned with midsummer sunrise, then in subsequent centuries, other circles and horseshoe shapes were built. Inside the henge the finished monument contained; an outside ring of wooden posts, a ring of upright stones with a continuous capstone circle, inside of which are huge stone trilithons. There are also several individual standing stones.

By this time, an amazing variety of alignments with lunar and solar events had been created, including equinoxes, solstices and eclipses! At a time when stone and antler tools were all people had to work with, this was a mighty undertaking spanning many generations. What was it for?

The central area can clearly accommodate a very big crowd of people. Recent archaeological studies have proved that rather than the modern day Summer Solstice festive gathering, evidence of Neolithic food litter suggests that Stonehenge (together with nearby Woodhenge) was really a midwinter meeting place associated with honouring the dead of the many clan groups that gathered there. In the surrounding landscape are a large number of burial mounds. In some of these barrows skeletons in the foetal position have been found, aligned to the midwinter sunrise or sunset. The symbolism is clear. The Winter Solstice, the shortest day, represents the death of the Sun. After three days of standstill the Sun is reborn with the lengthening days of the New Year and its strength starts to return. Perhaps the foetal position of the skeletons reflected the hope of rebirth from the earth's womb.

It appears that from these beginnings as a gathering to magically conjure the return of the sun, the Winter Solstice developed, partly into a festival to honour the dead, but just as importantly, as an annual gathering of peoples scattered over a large area who could assemble in one place, socialise and celebrate, as the evidence of great feasting (vast quantities of butchered pig bones) seems to indicate. Over centuries, meeting and celebration became the primary purpose of the Winter Solstice gathering, and creativity, decoration and myth-making reinforced much of its spiritual character,

The Winter Solstice had become a festival in its own right!

Neolithic Sacred Sites

The next few pages contain images of some of the many sacred sites all over Britain built by Neolithic people as observatories, temples, and meeting places. Many still attract visitors at the Winter Solstice, who gather to celebrate in their own way, perhaps not so very unlike how they did thousands of years ago.

STONEHENGE

Everyone is aware of the famous midsummer festival at Stonehenge, when hippies, Pagans and Druids gather to celebrate the Summer Solstice Sunrise. The Sun rises above the 'Heel stone' - from the word *haul* meaning Sun, in Old Welsh (the language nearest to ancient British). But turn your back upon this alignment and you are facing the Sunset at Winter Solstice!

Even more exciting, once every nineteen years you would have been able to witness the spectacular sight of the setting crescent New Moon visible in a window formed by the upper half of the Great Trilithon and the top of the lintels of the Sarcen stone circle as the sun sets between the uprights - but only if the sky is clear!

Unfortunately the stones have long since fallen in that part of the circle, so this spectacle is now lost forever.

Winter solstice

CALLANISH, Isle of Lewis, Scotland

Callanish was built between 2900 and 2600 BC in the form of a circle of 13 tall stones, with smaller stones forming a long double row avenue to the north, and shorter single stone rows to the east, south, and west. In the centre of the circle is a later burial chamber together with a taller standing stone. The whole monument is roughly the shape of a Celtic cross.

Callanish is called by some 'The Stonehenge of the North'.

The stones of Callanish incorporate many astronomical alignments within their structure: at various times it has been shown that the stones of the east row pointed to the rising of the constellation Pleiades; the west row aligns with sunsets of the spring and autumn equinoxes; at midsummer, the moon sets directly over Mt Clisham, when viewed along the avenue; sunset at the Winter Solstice aligns with the top of Tirga Mor; every 19 years, the moon skims along the horizon of the southern hills. There is also a chance you may see another amazing sight - the stones silhouetted against the startling colours of the Northern Lights.

A local legend tells of a magical white cow, who appeared at times of famine and gave freely to women who came to the stones, as long as they only took one pailful of milk each. One day a witch came with a sieve and tried to milk her dry, so she left Callanish and was never seen again.

Winter
Solstice

NEWGRANGE, Ireland

The great mound known as Brugh na Boinne (Newgrange) in County Meath, Ireland was constructed around 3,200BC, before Stonehenge and before the pyramids of Egypt.The circular mound is made of up to 450 huge boulders and an infinite number of smaller stones, roofed with grass. Inside there is a passageway with chambers. The outside wall is covered with bright white quartz stones, which make a stunning sight on top of the green hill.

Outside the entrance is a huge slab of stone carved with circles, spirals, dots, zig-zag lines and the Celtic triskel. These decorative carvings also appear inside the monument on other stones, several of which are concealed. Some archaeologists think there must have been a symbolic religious significance in this, but we don't know what the carvings might have meant.

At dawn on the Winter Solstice, the central chamber, where the love God Oenghus was said to live, is pierced by a single shaft of sunlight that enters through a little window above the entrance. The light strikes the stone slab at the back of the chamber, then widens and climbs upwards, illuminating the carvings in the chamber.

The light signifies the return of the Sun in the depths of winter, entering the being of the earth and promising light and warmth to come with the New Year.

WINTER
SOLSTICE

LONG MEG & HER DAUGHTERS

At the time of the Sun's lowest ebb, the shortest day, the dying Sun lights up the snow clad landscape with a last glory of blood red, marked by the stone called Long Meg. Tomorrow though, the Sun will rise anew, and the cycle will begin again with the waxing year.

At Little Salkeld, near Penrith, Cumbria, Long Meg stands with her Daughters about her, a magnificent stone circle, with Meg a tall outlier. Meg aligns from the entrance of the circle with the Winter Solstice sunset. On her side are spiral carvings representing the anti-clockwise shadow cast around her by the path of the Sun from midsummer to midwinter.

There are four quartz stones in the circle, which seem to mark alignments with Sunsets and Sunrises at the solstices and equinoxes. By standing outside the circle, behind the stones opposite the quartz marker stones, you may witness these events in front of you, beyond the quartz stone, on the other side of the circle.

A legend claims that if you walk around the circle and count the number of stones correctly, then put your ear to Long Meg, you will hear her whisper.

The name Long Meg is said to come from a local witch, Meg of Meldon, who lived nearby in the early 17th century.

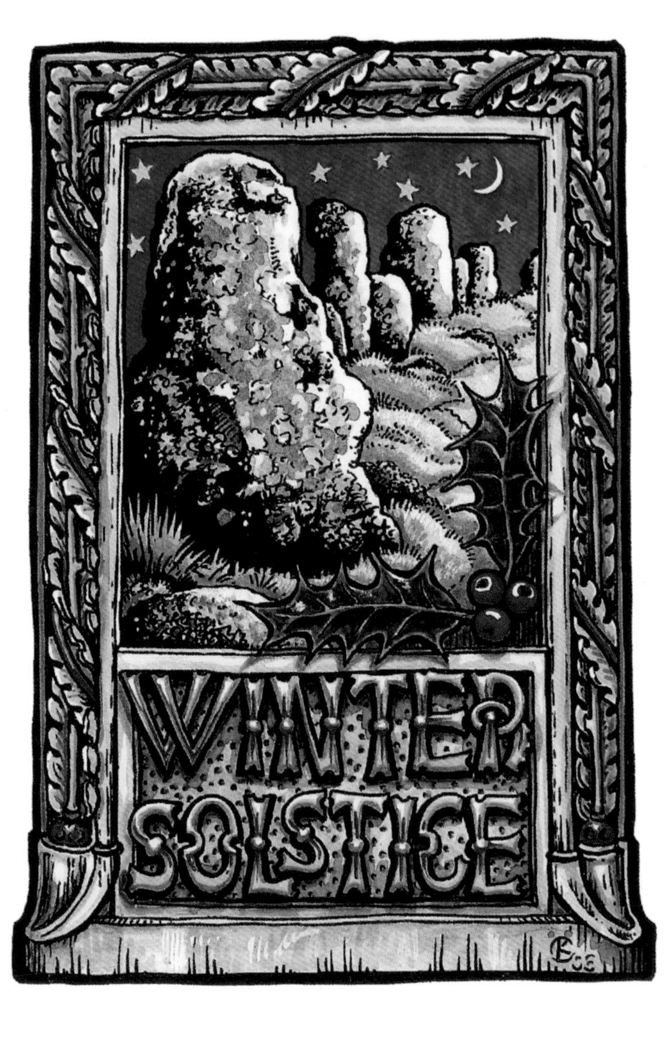
WINTER
SOLSTICE

AVEBURY

The village of Avebury, in Wiltshire, is surrounded by a huge circular banked and ditched henge, enclosing the largest stone circle in Western Europe, surrounding two further stone circles. It is part of a much larger sacred landscape which includes; West Kennet long barrow; Silbury Hill, the largest man made mound in Europe; The Sanctuary, a ritual site; Windmill Hill, a causewayed enclosure and Kennet Avenue, a stone flanked curved pathway linking the sites.

In the17th & 18th centuries much of the stone circle was systematically vandalised, many of the stones were broken up and reused as building materials.

Marking the northern entrance to the outer circle stands the gigantic 'Swindon stone' also called the 'Diamond stone', still in its original position, one of the few never to have been toppled. It is said that when the church clock strikes midnight, the Diamond stone crosses the road in search of its lost partner, which was destroyed in 1724.

Although the remaining stones as they appear today were mostly re-erected during the 1930s, Avebury gives the clear impression of an intact sacred site, retaining a strongly spiritual atmosphere.

In 2009 I visited Avebury on a frosty Winter Solstice afternoon, and was led around the North West sector of the circle up to the Diamond stone by a blackbird, while crows flew overhead.

The Swindon stone or Diamond stone, marking the northern entrance to Avebury stone circle.

Chapter 3

CELTIC WISDOM

Having found ways of working with the seasons and the cycles of nature to grow food and build communities, the ancient British people developed a social calendar based on the major events of the year; not only Winter Solstice, but planting, harvest, blessing a new building, births, coming of age, handfastings and deaths. On these occasions perhaps the elders appointed talented storytellers to lead rituals. They then may have imaginatively crafted tales to explain the festival's significance to the clan. Survival knowledge and clan history was woven into more and more elaborate legends; how to build a bridge; which wood makes the best tools; the deeds of a great chief; raiding parties; romantic liaisons between members of rival clans. To preserve the legends, storytellers would choose likely apprentices to train as successors - a priesthood was starting to develop!

As the Neolithic age progressed, several waves of Celtic peoples arrived in Britain from different parts of Europe, bringing their own legends. Eventually, over centuries, the traditions and mythology of many tribes became woven together. Great feats of memory became essential. The role of the trained priest then included advising chieftains, travelling between communities to settle disputes and maintaining the knowledge and history of all the peoples.

These priests became known as Druids.

OGHAM ~

The Druid Tree Alphabet

As time passed, Druids devised a system, part alphabet, part calendar or zodiac, able to be carved using simple notches onto wood or stone. Each character was a number and a letter. The consonants were time periods - mostly lunar months and the vowels were the solstices or equinoxes. Each symbol represents a tree or shrub, around which grew an extensive mythology, recording historical and religious stories, the uses of each tree both for craftwork and medicinally, and a divination system similar to the Tarot.
To the Celts the whole landscape was alive with meaning and wisdom - The wisdom of the trees.

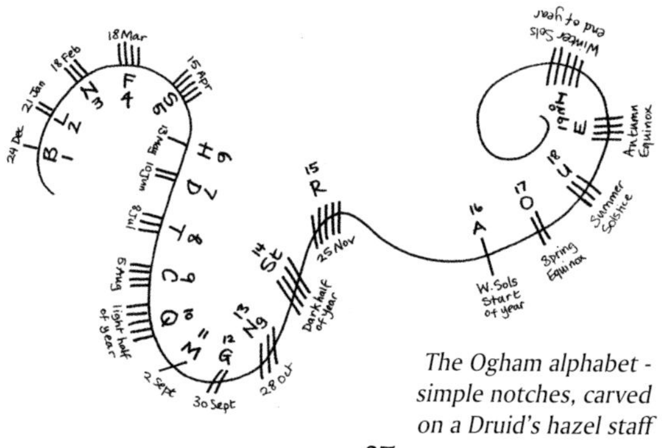

The Ogham alphabet - simple notches, carved on a Druid's hazel staff

TREE WHEEL

The Ogham Year

The outer ring of the Ogham Tree Wheel of the Year shows all the trees in their proper positions as far as possible; the solstices and equinoxes are shown between trees that include the actual date, and as close as possible to their proper positions.

Apple and Blackthorn form the inner ring as they rule the light and dark halves of the year respectively.

The centre of the wheel is the 'day' of 'a year and a day'. The Celtic lunar calendar reckoned the year as 13 months of 28 days = 364, so to complete the year an extra day was added - the 'year and a day' ruled by Mistletoe, the most magical of all.

The Winter Solstice is represented by two different trees. This is because each tree has a very specific meaning in the cycle of the year, but the Winter Solstice is the point at which the year turns, and the Old Year becomes the New Year, so while Yew is the sentinel guarding the ending of the Old Year, Scots Pine is the signpost pointing the way for the journey into the New Year.

Two roles - two trees.

Scotts Pine
Birch
Ash
Gorse
Alder
Willow
Hawthorn
Heather
Oak
Hazel
Aspen
Ivy
Wheatstraw
Elder
WINTER
SOLSTICE
24th Dec-20th Jan
21st Jan-17th Feb
18th Feb-17th Mar
Spring Equinox
18th Mar-14th Apr
15th Apr-12th May
13th May-9th Jun
Summer Solstice
10th Jun-7th Jul
8th Jul-4th Aug
5th Aug-1st Sep
Autumnal Equinox
30th Sep-27th Oct
28th Oct-24th Nov
25th Nov-22nd Dec
IOHO
AILM
BEITH
LUIS
NION
ONN
FEARN
SAILLE
HUATH
UR
DUIR
TINNE
COLL
MUIN
EADHA
GORT
NGETAL
RUIS
BLACKTHORN - DARK HALF OF THE YEAR
APPLE - LIGHT HALF OF THE YEAR
QUERT
STRAIF
MISTLETOE
23rd DEC

YEW

A Guardian at the Threshold

The Yew tree is the symbol for the Winter Solstice at the end of the Old Year and represents ideas of regeneration and protection of the spirit of the dead in preparation for rebirth. Perhaps most appropriately, Yew is the longest lived of all native trees. A Yew tree in St Cynogg's Churchyard, Defynogg, Powys, Wales has been tested and found to be at least 5,000 years old!

After many centuries, the Yew's central trunk becomes hollow, and new growth may spring up within the dead trunk, appearing like a new tree. Sometimes the drooping branches, where they touch the earth, may root and send up new growth to eventually become a ring of young trees - the new generation, but also an extension of the original tree. Yew illustrates perfectly the continuing cycles of life, death and rebirth.

All parts of the Yew are poisonous, in fact the word *toxic*, meaning poisonous, is derived from the latin name for the Yew – *taxus*. Though poisoning may result in death, the Yew tree growing in a churchyard is regarded as the guardian of the spirits of the dead buried there . Many old tales tell of a root of the Yew growing into the mouths of corpses to preserve them until rebirth or the day of judgement.

Yew
21st Dec
Winter
Solstice
end of year
Ioho

SCOTS PINE

A Signpost into the New Year

Scots Pine is the symbol for the Winter Solstice at the start of the New Year, representing ideas of guidance and prediction, pointing the way as a signpost.

Scots Pine is the only true native pine, thought to be the first tree to establish after the ice age. The mature young tree is conical in shape, but as it ages the lower branches die off to leave a bare trunk and the higher growth becomes flattened to leave a distinctive silhouette. The cones can be used to predict weather, as when the atmosphere is damp, before rain, the cones will shut tightly, opening only when the air dries indicating better conditions to come.

The tall pine tree stands above the distractions of life, which crowd around at the foot of the tree among the leaf litter. He sees far into the distance and points the way, aloof and guiding, protecting and reviving, but above all far seeing. Scots Pines were often planted in small groups of two or three on 'sighting points', either along ley lines or on tumuli, and may have been used to navigate great distances across the ancient landscape, following from one signpost to another at elevated points on the horizon.

Scots Pine
22nd Dec
Winter
Solstice
start of year
Ailm

Chapter 4 - MISTLETOE

'All-Heal'

Looking up into trees, bare of leaves in the depth of winter, it is difficult not to be fascinated by the sometimes huge bunches of Mistletoe, growing out of many an Apple tree, Poplar, Lime or Ash, or sometimes even the Druids' sacred tree, the Oak.

The Druids believed that Mistletoe itself was too sacred to be given a name, but they called it 'All-heal' because of its powerful medicinal properties. A magical plant, not of the earth but growing between earth and sky, so that it forms a mystic link between them, Mistletoe is the 'Other', representing liminal space, that which is neither one thing nor the other, but which is the point of stillness between. At the Winter Solstice, Mistletoe represents the threshold between the end of the old year and the start of the new.

To the Celts, liminal space was the place where magic could happen, and all such places were held as sacred - dawn and dusk, the meeting of day and night; the sea strand or shore where land meets the sea; gateways and thresholds, all had magical power. They were the separation between the physical and spiritual worlds, where access from one to the other was possible.

WINTER
SOLSTICE

THE GOLDEN SICKLE

The Roman author Pliny the Elder wrote of Gaulish Druids in the first century AD;

“The Druids – that is what they call their magicians – hold nothing more sacred than the Mistletoe and the tree on which it is growing, provided it is an Oak.... Mistletoe is rare and it is gathered with great ceremony,.... using a native word that means 'healing all things,' ... A priest arrayed in white vestments climbs the tree and, with a golden sickle, cuts down the mistletoe, which is caught in a white cloak... praying to a god to render his gift propitious to those on whom he has bestowed it. They believe that mistletoe given in drink will impart fertility to any animal that is barren and that it is an antidote to all poisons”

It was believed that if the mistletoe was cut with an iron blade, or if it touched the ground when dropped from the tree, its magical properties would be lost.

Though Pliny fails to record the time of year when the ceremony took place, it is almost certain that it would often happen at mid-winter, when the berries are ripe. These days Mistletoe is an essential element of decoration in the home at mid-winter, and the fertility aspect of Druid belief still finds echoes in the custom of ‘kissing under the Mistletoe’.

IN A WHITE ROBE THE DRUID PREIST ASCENDS THE OAK TREE
AND CUTS THE MISTLETOE WITH A GOLDEN SICKLE
IT IS CAUGHT IN A WHITE CLOAK

THE KISSING BOUGH

Every Berry Means a Kiss

As part of mid-winter Yuletide celebrations to this day, it is often customary to make a 'Kissing Bough'. This can vary from a single branch of Mistletoe to an elaborate decoration using two hoops, one thrust through the other and bound around with evergreens, holly and ivy, and with apples specially reserved for the occasion. Inside are hung representations of male and female figures, and other brightly coloured baubles. At the bottom a bunch of Mistletoe is carefully tied, and the whole tableau is suspended in the middle of the room, the centre of attention. Every berry on the mistletoe bears the promise of a kiss, an echo of the ancient fertility rite, and for every kiss given or taken, a berry must be removed. When all the berries are gone, the kissing has to stop!

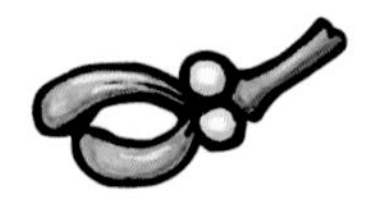

The transition from the old year to the new, from the dying to the reborn, is enabled by the love, fertility and healing that is represented by the many properties of Mistletoe. A truly magical plant!

The Kissing Bough
The Kissing Bough
The Kissing Bough
The Kissing Bough

BRING MISTLETOE IN

"Pass the jug round, let joy be unbound
The fire burns brightly and gay,
The drums steady sound and thunder the ground
To welcome our dancing day.
The Robin is glad, no folk should be sad,
Be merry and joyful I say,
Cast out fear of sin and bring Mistletoe in
To brighten the darkest of days"

From 'Wailey Wailer',
the Whimple Carol, from South East Devon.
Thanks to Jim Causley - from his CD 'Dumnonia'

BRING MISTLETOE IN
TO BRIGHTEN THE DARKEST OF DAYS

Chapter 5

EVOLUTION OF LEGENDS AND CUSTOMS

Roman Saturnalia

During the Roman conquest of Britain, Gaius Seutonius Paulinus led an army to Mona (Anglesey) in 60 or 61AD, massacring the Druids in their last stronghold and destroying the sacred groves where they performed rituals. It is said that all the Druids perished, but it is unlikely that such a powerful intellectual priesthood would not plan for the possibility of defeat.

After a campaign lasting nearly twenty years, the Romans had finally established their authority over much of Britain. Many Roman soldiers came from previously conquered parts of Europe. After completing service with the legions, some eventually married British women and settled, becoming integrated into British life. They also brought with them legends and beliefs from their homelands which became woven together with older British traditions. It was the Roman way to incorporate native belief systems rather than impose their own culture immediately; it was easier to get newly subjugated peoples to co-operate if they continued to follow familiar customs. Gradually Roman and British Gods and legends became intertwined. Many older Gods were given additional names of Roman deities sharing similar characteristics (Sulis Minerva of the spring at Bath,

Belenus Apollo associated with the Sun). As early as 55BC Julius Caesar had written that Mercury was the most popular God in Gaul and Britain - as Lugus (Celtic Lugh) he may well have been!

In 410AD, the Romans finally left Britain with their empire collapsing. Belief systems in Britain may not have changed dramatically, and some festivals, including the Winter Solstice continued to be observed as before, though with a more Romanesque flavour.

The main Roman midwinter festival was Saturnalia. Saturn was associated with agriculture and plenty, also with passing time. He is depicted as an old man wielding a scythe, which finds echoes in the more modern 'Father Time'. Saturnalia lasted from 17th to the 24th December, when in order to avert the 'crisis' of the Winter Solstice, when the death of the Sun could otherwise spread calamity, the normal social order was reversed; the 'World turned upside-down', when masters would wait on their servants and festivities were overseen by a 'Lord of Misrule' whose job it was to organise theatrical and musical entertainments.

Much of the imagery of Saturnalia survives into comparatively recent times, with echoes right up to the present day: the Twelve Days of Christmas season of merriment; election of Boy Bishops, a clerical version of the Lord of Misrule, which still takes place in several cathedral schools; Guising and Mumming traditions.

The Other Roman Midwinter Festival

Originally the Indo-Persian God Mithra was known over a widespread area from the eastern Mediterranean to India. He was a Sun God in the Indian Vedic scriptures written around 1500BC, who bestowed health, wealth and food and was the bringer of fire.

In Asia minor and the Near East, at least as far back as 650BC, Mithra's cult concentrated on aspects of his legend which bore remarkable similarities to Jesus Christ's; born of a virgin mother at midwinter and a teacher with twelve followers who sacrificed himself for the good of all people.

In the Greco-Roman world Mithras was called "Sol Invictus" - "The Unconquered Sun", and was the mediator between earth and the heavens. The appeal to the Roman legions of an unconquered God led to their adopting him as their patron and spreading his following throughout the Empire. Here the cult of Mithras developed as a seven-fold initiation, his mysteries celebrated in underground temples with the iconic image of Mithras killing a bull.

On 25th December the Romans celebrated Dies Natalis Invicta Solis – the Birth of the Unconquered Sun God. It is not hard to find the parallels; at the Winter Solstice the Sun has lost its strength and 'dies', after three days, it is reborn as the Unconquered Sun. The twists and turns of comparative mythology show how a single phenomenon (the Winter Solstice) can evolve in diverse cultures into a fascinating variety of interpretations and coincidences.

'The Unconquered Sun';
'Sol Invictus' gave his name
to the Roman
midwinter festival of
'Dies Natalis Invicta Solis'
'the birthday of the
Unconquered Sun'
on 25th December.

Mithras, patron God
of the Roman legions,
who was portrayed
killing a bull.

THE DARK AGES;

Heathens and Christian missionaries

After the Romans left Britain, several groups of settlers from what is now Germany and Scandinavia began to arrive with varying degrees of menace. Vikings had a fearsome reputation, but Saxons, Angles and some Danes mostly traded peacefully, making their homes here, becoming farmers and melding with the existing population. They brought with them a new pantheon: Odin/Woden, Thor/Thunor, Loki, Frejya, Frigg, etc. some of whom eventually gave their names to days of the week: Wednesday = Woden's day, Thursday = Thor's day, Friday = Frigg's day.

During this period, Christian missionaries also began to reach Britain, bringing the message of a new Unconquered Sun; Jesus, the Son of God. But while the incoming Heathens were fairly happy to coexist with whatever deities and festivals they found in Britain, these new Christians were on a mission! It was their task to overthrow the old ways and replace them with a new religion. To achieve this, monasteries and churches were built, many on existing Pagan sacred sites; native Gods and Goddesses were translated into saints e.g. Brigid / St. Bridget; existing festivals were overlaid with new Holy Days. Not only did this approach help to promote the new religion, but enabled some of the older beliefs to live on in a somewhat informal way.

Over time many native beliefs became demonised or were dismissed as 'superstitions', but when the date of Christ's birth was settled and its festival, Christmas, established, the 25th December was chosen, the birthday of the Sun!

Brigid was the Irish Goddess of healing and midwifery for both people and animals, also of smithcraft, poetry and of the hearthfire. She has many wells and springs dedicated to her. Brigid is thought to be an aspect of Danu, the Irish Mother Goddess.
Christian monks took the ancient figure of the mother goddess and grafted her name and functions onto her Christian counterpart.
As St Bridget of Kildare she cured many diseases by means of water which she caused to miraculously appear. St Brigit of Sweden had a vision of the Nativity of Jesus, in some accounts was transported by angels to act as midwife to the Virgin Mary. St Bridget is the patron saint of among others: babies, blacksmiths, dairymaids, midwives, poets and watermen.

The Green Man

Look carefully in many Norman cathedrals and churches all over England, and carved in stone it is possible to see the head of a man mysteriously emerging from the foliage sprouting from his mouth and covering his face. The masons of medieval times paid homage to deities and powers other than those to whom the churches were dedicated. These foliate heads were given the name 'Green Man' by folklorist Lady Raglan as recently as 1940 and it was believed that by the power of the Green Man, new life returned to the land each spring. Fertility God or simply decoration, the Green Man holds a strange fascination for many people to this day.

Deck The Halls With Boughs Of Holly

The gathering of evergreens to decorate homes at the Winter Solstice has probably happened for at least two thousand years. Deciduous trees lose their leaves in winter, appearing to die for several months; the spirit of the tree, or life force, being lost with the foliage. So it seems that those who keep their leaves throughout the winter somehow magically retain that life force.

Holly is doubly blessed at this time of year, covered in bright red berries - the fruit that may give rise to new life if they fall onto fertile soil and are allowed to grow.

Red is the colour if life; the colour of blood, the essential liquid that enables the bodies of creatures to maintain life. The red berries of Holly, appearing like drops of blood, represent that precious life-giving liquid.

By bringing evergreen holly into the home, the life force is captured for the benefit of all who live there, protecting them from weakness and death that may come to them as it has come to the Sun. Perhaps the red berries also recall the colours of the sky at Sunset and again at Sunrise, reinforcing the certainty that, having died, the Sun will return again after the Solstice.

Even in modern times, with artificial decorations so freely available, many still decorate their homes with at least a little bunch of holly, or a holly wreath on the front door!

WINTER SOLSTICE GREEN MAN

As the land sleeps at the deepest dark of the year, though all seems still and quiet, there are creatures stirring in the night. Not every animal will sleep away the winter, but most will only stray abroad when need is great, for it is a cold and hungry time for those who are awake.

On this night, the longest of all, another force is stirring. The life of the land is at its lowest ebb, but even now there is a promise of new life to come. The berries and seeds which will grow in the spring shine brightly in the hedgerow, and the Green Man laughs as he wishes us a Merry Solstice.

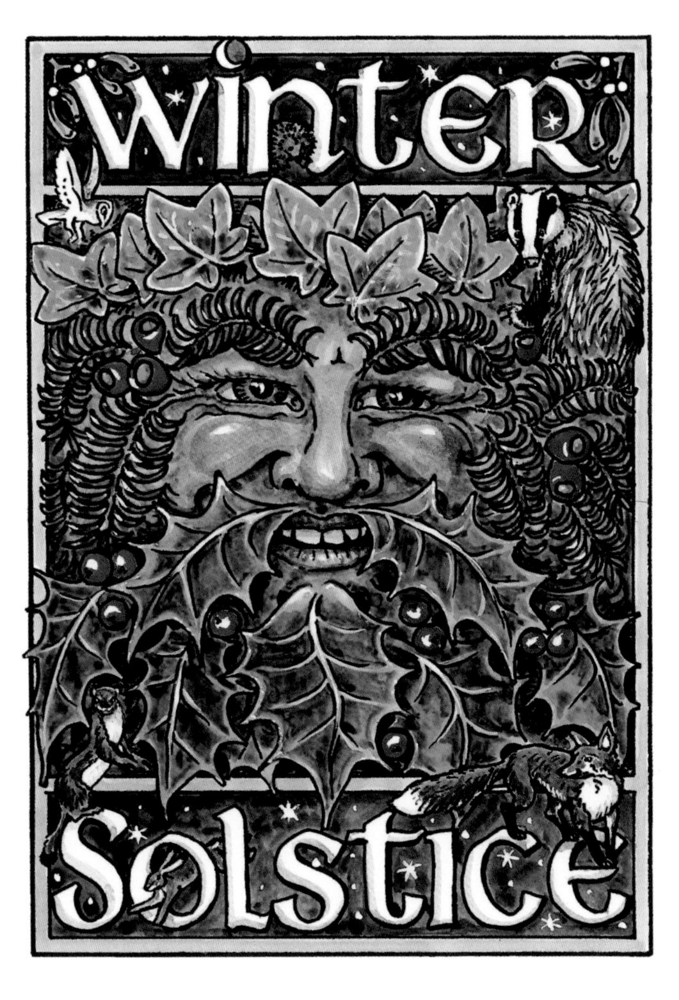
Winter
Solstice

The Holly King & The Oak King

The lagend of the Holly King and the Oak King tells of two brothers who fight a ritualised battle for dominance every Summer and Winter Solstice. At Yule the Oak King is triumphant, and rules until the Summer Solstice, when at the height of his power he sacrifices himself allowing the Holly King to take his turn. The Holly King will reign until he too must relinquish his power at the time of his greatest glory. The year is therefor ruled by each brother at the time they are most full of life - the deciduous Oak during its most vigorous growing phase, and the evergreen Holly as he approaches maximum potency with the ripening berries. This legend teaches that the wheel of the year is held in ballance with the promise of eternal and continuous life force.

The kingship of the Holly is that of the sacrificial king, the Sun King who dies and is reborn at the Winter Solstice. His blood is the red berries that ripen in winter and are used for Yuletide decorations, because they also represent light warmth and fire.

Holly was used for decoration at the Roman midwinter feast of Saturnalia, as it was said that the club which the God Saturn wielded was made of holly. So when the date of Christmas was finalised at the same time of year, people continued to use holly and it became part of Christmas imagery.

YULE
THE REIGN OF THE HOLLY KING
THE REIGN OF THE OAK KING

The Mummers Are Coming!

As the long dark nights drew in and Christmas was approaching, Mummers with flaming torches traipsed through snowy Yuletide lanes, led by a 'Whiffler' to sweep the path and clear the way for the Merry Actors, bringing the magic of old to those with open hearts.

Their play is the ancient story of the battle between 'St George' and the evil 'Black Prince of Paradise', where one or both are slain, only to be revived again by the antics of a 'Quack Doctor'. Any number of other characters appears, but inevitably it all ends with a song and a collection to provide the Mummers with a well earned drink.

Once again the age-old theme of the death and rebirth of the Sun is reflected in the story of 'death and regeneration' that is the central core of most midwinter mummers plays.

Meanwhile, out in the snow, badgers leave their warm 'set' briefly to forage for food, scraping away the snow in search of tasty morsels. They are watched carefully by a hare, sheltering in her 'form'. She has no cosy hole to sleep away the winter, so must find what comfort she can in the harsh December weather.

DECEMBER

Mummers at Christmas

Two hundred years ago the population of England numbered fewer than ten million, most of whom lived in villages. In the depths of winter, when the land was frozen and too hard to plough, working people would try to make an honest crust by their skills as entertainers. Mummers went out visiting the houses of the well to do. Often they were expected, so that after their performance they would be rewarded with food, drink and perhaps a small amount of money, and a good time was had by all.

Mumming is an ancient tradition still regularly re-enacted throughout the UK, though today, the performances are usually outside pubs with money collected for charity. Although its origins are lost in the mists of time, characters such as the Saracen, Turk, or the 'Black Prince of Paradise', suggest they could go back as far the Crusades. It's pretty clear that Mummers plays were once mainstream popular culture; texts were produced by local printers in large quantities in Chapbooks, Almanacks or Broadsides. Although the earliest full play text dates back only to 1738, references to mumming, masking and disguising at Christmas are innumerable during the medieval period and it is likely that the tradition is very old.

The Doctor pulls a tooth from Prince George, who is attended by Moll Finney and the Foreman, while Tom Fool/ Big Head, Bold Slasher and Humpty Jack watch.
From the Stoneleigh Christmas Play by Coventry Mummers.

Here We Come A-Wassailing

All over England and Wales, groups of Wassailers would also be out collecting to help finance Christmas. But what is Wassailing? The word Wassail comes from the old Norse 'Waes Hael' meaning 'be of good health'. Food, drink and money were sought in return for a song and a blessing. Perhaps a Wassail bowl would be offered by the visitors, containing a spiced cider or ale drink, said to confer good health and luck for the coming year.

"Here we come a-wassailing 'long with our Lucy Green,
And here we come a wandering as fair to be seen."

Parties of carollers from Camborne, Cornwall, were accompanied by a young girl dressed in evergreens, and known as Lucy Green. Perhaps representing, as evergreen Christmas decorations are said to, the eternal spirit of life preserved over winter awaiting rebirth in the coming year.

This might not seem unusual, were it not that in Baltic countries, St Lucy's Day is widely celebrated. There a young girl dressed in white wearing a crown of candles on her head, symbolises purity and the triumph of light over darkness that embodies most Winter Solstice celebrations. St Lucy's Day is December 13th, a date capable of being interpreted as the Winter Solstice depending on how relationships between Julian and Gregorian calendars are interpreted.

WASSAILING
HERE WE COME A-
'LONG WITH OUR
THANK YOU
LUCY GREEN

Apple Orchard Wassailing

A Wassail blessing would wish health and happiness on the household visited, also the farm and its animals or crops, especially on apple orchards. Apple Orchard Wassailing was widespread throughout Kent & Sussex; Herefordshire, Worcestershire & Gloucestershire and Devon & Somerset up until the middle of the 20th century, when it nearly died out. In the later part of that century, folk enthusiasts, inspired by a few recorded songs, started to reawaken the old custom, and since the millenium it has been taken up by Community Orchards and Cider farms too. Now there are hundreds of Wassails all over the place!

The Wassailers might process carrying burning torches to the orchard after dark. Cider would be poured on the roots, returning the blood of the tree, apple juice, to revive and reawaken its spirit. Toast would be placed in the branches for the robins, the guardian spirits of the trees, though these days some tie ribbons to the branches and make a wish for a blessing for the New Year. A chant and a song would be followed by a deafening noise - either shotguns fired into the branches or the assembled crowd would bang pots and pans and shout and holloa to scare away the evil spirits that might otherwise blight the next year's crop. Then everyone may share a toast to the trees and each other by drinking from a three handled Wassail bowl, passed around from hand to hand, before returning to the house (pub) for an evening of merriment.

Wassail

Helping to Revive the Sun

In modern times, while popular Christmas is the distant descendant of the ancient festival of the Winter Solstice, there is much imagery that is still held in common.

We decorate our homes or send cards with pictures of evergreen branches – holly, ivy, mistletoe – to maintain the spirit of life till the New Year. We hang fairy lights on a pine tree; though the 'Christmas tree' is said to be imported by Prince Albert from German tradition in the mid 19th century, remember the Scots Pine of the Druid Ogham? While lights and candles are surely practicalities to brighten the dark time of year, could these be echoes of the rituals of sympathetic magic employed to revive the dead Sun? Fires and lights, flaming torches and candles all show the Sun what it needs to do and encourages it to reawaken after its three days stand-still at the death of the Sun.

Before matches were invented, people lit fires using a tinder box ('tinder' from the Ogham name for holly – Tinne), and household fires were rarely allowed to go out as rekindling was a lengthy process. During the Christmas period it was considered incredibly bad luck to allow fire to leave the home, so although at other times it would be thought neighbourly to give a light to someone in need, at the time when the Sun dies, this was never done, lest the fire was lost forever!

So as you hang your fairy lights and light your candles this Yuletide, reflect on their ancient purpose and spare a moment to think of how many people have done this for how many thousands of years before you!

I hope you have enjoyed the ideas and artwork in this little book. If you would like to see more, many of these images are available as greetings cards and mounted prints from:

www.hedinghamfair.co.uk

or, for an illustrated catalogue, contact:

email: info@hedinghamfair.co.uk
Tel: 01787 462731

Other books by Karen Cater
also available from Hedingham Fair:

OGHAM SKETCHBOOK
a Diary of Tree Lore and Spiritual Growth

SPIRIT OF THE HARE
in Folklore, Mythology and the Artist's Landscape

WINTER SOLSTICE

ROLLRIGHT STONES

Near Little Rollright, Oxfordshire, stands 'The King's Men', a late Neolithic ceremonial stone circle, part of the Rollright stones site. Just across the road is the 'King Stone' a single standing stone surrounded by metal railings and down the lane and across another field is a group of five stones, thought to be part of a Long Barrow, leaning together, known as the 'Whispering Knights'.

The King's Men are 77 rough stones described by the antiquarian William Stukeley as being "corroded like worm eaten wood, by the harsh Jaws of Time". Dowsers have recorded powerful reactions within the circle, often described as concentric rings of energy, though many say they are in fact a spiral.

Spiral dances can be included in Winter Solstice rituals to imitate the path of the Sun as its shadow follows the annual cycle from summer to winter (like the spiral carved on the flank of Long Meg), and back again to summer. Dancers hold hands in a long line and starting in a wide arc, dance a spiral path inwards towards the centre. Then, changing direction, dance back outwards between the lines of following dancers, until they return to the outside of the spiral, and may form a ring before ending. This dance can be performed to encourage the Sun in its rebirth and renewal. The centre of the dance, where the direction reverses, represents the Winter Solstice.